MW00694983

Blended Learning

"A Concise Guide for Mixing Technology with Instruction in all Classrooms"

Brent A. Bogan, Ed.S.

Matthew R. Ogles, M.Ed

Published by UCM Management,
P.O. Box 12505
Murfreesboro, TN 37129

Copyright © 2016. All rights reserved. Except as permitted under
the U.S. Copyright Act of 1976, no part of this publication may be
reproduced, distributed, or transmitted in any form or by any means
or stored in a database or retrieval system, without the prior written
permission of the publisher.

This publication is designed to provide competent and reliable
information regarding the subject matter covered. The authors and
publisher specifically disclaim any liability that is incurred from the
use or application of the contents of this book.

All web links in this book are correct as of the publication date but
may have become inactive or otherwise modified since the time of
publication.

Printed in the United States of America.

About the Authors

Brent Bogan is the founder of the popular professional development company, Unconventional Teaching (www.UnconventionalTeaching.com). Unconventional Teaching workshops specialize in topics such as classroom management, assessment strategies, the flipped classroom/education technology, and creating entertaining and memorable lessons for students.

He has been a classroom educator since 2006. Bogan currently serves as a vice-principal at a high performing elementary school and was formerly a high school teacher and dean of students. Bogan has taught a wide variety of different subjects, including Sociology, Government, History, and Geography. He also has experience as an educator in a wide spectrum of different grade levels.

Bogan is native to the small farming community of Sabina, Ohio. Brent currently resides with his wife and son in Tennessee. Bogan attended Middle Tennessee State University, where he received a Bachelor of Science Degree in Geosciences, a Master of Education Degree in Administration & Supervision, and an Education Specialist Degree with an emphasis in Curriculum & Instruction. In his free time, he enjoys playing guitar, spending time with his family, and traveling.

Matthew R. Ogles is a founder of the educational company Unconventional Classroom in which he strives to improve teachers' craft to help them reach every student that they encounter. He graduated from Middle Tennessee State University with a Bachelor of Arts Degree in History and a Masters of Education Degree in Administration and Supervision.

He has been an educator for several years in the state of Tennessee, where he has taught U.S. History, Government, Geography, Health, and World History while serving as the head of the Social Studies Department at his school. He has consistently had some of the highest growth margins on state mandated tests with his students, while keeping his class exciting and fun. Matthew currently resides in a small town in Middle Tennessee with his wife and co-founder of Unconventional Classroom, Rachael.

Contents

Chapter 1

The Students of Today

When I was a kid, I used to listen to stories of the "good ole days," and just sit in a state of wonder thinking, "How did the world change so much since then?!" Relatives would sometimes tell of a time before color television or before television in general! They'd tell of the days when school was just one small building and just one teacher in that building. It was always amazing to me that everything had changed so much since they were my young age; it was like they lived in a different world! Now that I'm older, that sense of wonder still sticks with me, but now, I'm in the opposite seat. I sit back now and wonder how the world has changed so much since I was a youngster! I now know exactly how my relatives felt all those years; it's like I live in a different world from the kids now. I see areas of once farmland developed into apartment complexes. I see shopping malls where carnivals used to be held each year. I see cars that don't even need gas to run. I see televisions as flat as a book when they

1

used to basically be part of the furniture! One of the most noticeable changes I see on a day-to-day basis is that everyone you meet has a cell phone in their hand.

When I was a kid, cell phones were things you'd see in spy movies or stories of a distant future, but now they are as commonplace as a pair of eyeglasses. From the way that some people are attached to them, you might think they were as necessary as eyeglasses, too! But here's the thing, we know the world is a changing place, and it's our job as teachers to adapt to that. Think about it, what if our teachers growing up had refused to use the first computers? We'd be lost in a fully computer oriented world. The same logic applies for us as teachers now. We must use the up and coming technology in our classrooms to prepare the students for the real world. We have to implement it on a daily basis and turn our classrooms into a blended learning environment. So how do we do it? We must first learn more about the students of today and how they function; we must learn about the 21st century learners.

21st century learners are the generation after the millennials. They're constantly changing and developing so much that a nickname has not yet been formally given to them. However, despite not having an official nickname, it is well known why they are constantly changing...technology and the Internet. So much of their present life, and soon to be future, is technology and online based. Think about it. When you see a teenager, what's the first thing you also see? Right! Their cell phone! 21st century learners are reliant on technology and their cell phone. According to researcher Amanda Lenhart with the Pew Research Center, 75% of teenagers have access to a cell phone.[1] Even if they don't have access, they're still using technology elsewhere because 92% of teens report going online daily. That's 92 out of 100 teenagers online every single day, and these numbers just continue to rise. So what does this tell us? It tells us that if 92% of our class is integrated into something, then we HAVE to be using it in our classroom! [1]

Let's break down these learners a step further on what they use online access for. At least 71% of teens use at least one social media site, such as Facebook, Instagram, or Twitter. [1] This tells us they love being socially connected. If that high of a percentage of students are using such platforms, should we as teachers not be getting on board as well? Of course we should! There are lots of ways to use these networks in your classroom. I know so many teachers who use twitter to tweet out assignments or Facebook to give updates to parents. It's vital to meet the students at a halfway point on all their technology needs!

21st century learners aren't restricted to just cellphones and social media. 81% of teenagers age 13 to 17 have access to a video game console as well. [1] Back in my generation (here we go again, haha) only the nerdy kids played a lot of video games, but now the flood gates have opened and almost every kid plays video games. This is just another aspect of technology usage that students of this generation use, and therefore, we should consider including in our lessons.

Not every learner uses a smartphone or has video games, but to fill in the missing gaps, we have a whopping 87% who use desktop or laptop computers. [1] This can cover social media as well as video games, but can go even further. There are so many design programs available that students use. They can be creating music, making movies, or designing programs. The possibilities for what a student can use a computer for are endless, and almost all teenagers have access to one. Once again, if they are so integrated into technology, then we have no choice but to use computers in our classroom. By doing this, it makes the information more relevant and helps to prepare them for the world we are pushing them into.

What this boils down to is that the students in our classrooms live in a different generation than the one we grew up in. They have technology around them at all times. Whether it is their phone, video games, computer, or online access; they are surrounded by technology almost all of the time. It's the world they live in and it will most certainly be part of their future. Yes, there is that small percentage of students who do not have technology access readily available, but that only means that we need to step up our game as educators just one step further. If they don't have it at home, then we must teach it to them at school. If technology is a major part of the current times and also the future, it must be utilized in every classroom. This is where Blended Learning is born.

1. Lenhart. Amanda. Pew Research Center. April 2015. "Teen. Social Media and Technology

Overview 2015

Chapter 2

What is Blended

Learning?

There's nothing more refreshing than biting into a freshly picked, ripe strawberry in the warmth of late spring. The delicious scents that the strawberries give off can bring you back to some of your favorite moments as a child. The sweetness of a banana can be a great supplement to a breakfast or a recovery food after a tough workout. The potassium is excellent for helping bodies break down and use carbohydrates. Both are excellent and healthy foods. When you blend and combine the Vitamin K from the strawberries and the Potassium from the banana, you not only have a very healthy snack, but you have a taste explosion like no other. While strawberries and bananas are a tasty treat by themselves, blending the two together is a more effective way to receive your nutrients all at once and a strawberry-banana smoothie is delicious.

Strawberries and bananas are not the only two fruits that blend well together. According to the Mintel Intelligence

Group in July of 2012, the smoothie industry is a 2.4 billion dollar a year industry.[2] There are entire franchises that have based their business model around the idea of mixing various fruits and vegetables together to create healthy drink mixes.

Along with the enhancement of fruits and vegetables being combined, a mixed or differentiated menu of lessons can also have an equally positive reaction for student learning and engagement. Blended Learning is the combination of the integration of technology based learning along with face-to-face learning. Throughout this book, it will become apparent that the ratio of the mix of traditional direct learning and the inclusion of technology differs from one classroom to another. Blended learning has had many different names throughout the years, including "technology mediated instruction," "mixed-mode instruction," and even "web-enhanced instruction," but they ultimately all include the combination of the traditional, physical classroom instruction mixed with hands-on technology instruction.

One of the key features of blended learning is that it allows for more individualized learning. Students can be actively engaged in a lesson on an iPad, computer, or other electronic device, while the teacher can work with isolated groups to directly teach to students and to check for understanding. The teacher can circulate throughout the classroom and spend time with each small group to ensure that learning is taking place and to assist with any questions that the students may have. As the interests and hobbies of students are evolving over time and as students are becoming continuously surrounded by technology, teachers must also evolve in the ways that they instruct students. Blended learning is an excellent way to incorporate technology, which will spark student interest and engagement.

Another method of blended learning could involve a direct instruction lesson for the entire class, and after the lecture or discussion, the students could begin using technology as a supplemental material for the lesson or to assess a student's understanding of the content that has just been taught.

Because all students learn at a different pace, another option for blended learning could be introducing new lessons to students who are more advanced in their learning or for the students who haven't completely grasped ahold of a concept. For example, they may have the option of listening/viewing previous lessons to help reinforce the learning. With the instructor also being in the room to work with small groups or to assist with any questions that the students may have, the students have the security net of independently learning on a technological device at a pace that's comfortable to them while also getting feedback and reassurance from a live teacher in the classroom. The discovery, investigation, and those "light bulb going off above the head" moments are all still possible for students with the blended model of teaching. In fact, the blended model provides more opportunities and depth for all of those things to take place. With the heavy incorporation of technology, students are not left behind in a classroom that doesn't keep up with the world in which our students live in, which is surrounded by technology.

There is wide spread speculation that in the near future, the idea of tangible/physical textbooks may be a thing of the past. As more and more schools are introducing tablet devices and with several technology grants available to schools, many textbooks and publishers may be moving towards placing their textbooks in a digital format. With this potential move, students would no longer carry around excessively heavy backpacks full of six or seven textbooks along with their other supplies. Instead, all of the textbooks would be condensed into a tablet or device that is used for all subject areas.

With the possibility of textbooks being completely digital in the future, there is perhaps nothing that will prepare students for tomorrow than a blended learning model. The idea of blended learning is to not completely make learning

100% about virtual learning and technology. The concept is to not eliminate the physical classroom. Instead, it's designed to allow the physical classroom to be conducive to more creativity and openness with the concept of introducing a wide variety of technological education methods. Throughout this book, the three main types of blended learning will be explained. The three types of blended learning include: face-to-face driver, online driver, and rotation. To a teacher who is already familiar with the flipped learning method, there are several patterns that are similar with the blended model; however, the greatest difference is that the majority of technology use is within the classroom instead of being viewed at home. Because the inability for some students to access the internet and to find a computer are the greatest hindrance of the flipped model, with the blended model, schools provide the internet access along with the technology needed.

For schools that have difficulty funding tablets or computers, a fantastic place to begin seeking funds to purchase is donorschoose.org. This website is designed for schools in communities that have low funding for technological needs, and there are numerous donors who are looking to help those schools.

A second option for seeking funding for technology is through PledgeCents.com. This is another platform for helping your classroom or school meet its financial need for the inclusion of technology, which is not only necessary for blended learning, but is necessary for computer-based state testing in many states.

Once funding is completed for your classroom, you are ready to begin with Blended Learning, but you will need to know choose if you want to do a face-to-face, online, or a rotation driven classroom. Each method has its advantages, and in the next three chapters, each model will be explained in greater detail to help you choose what is best for your classroom!

2. Mintel. *U.S. SMOOTHIE MARKET SLURPS UP $2 BILLION IN SALES*. Rep. N.p., 21

Feb. 2007. Web. 1 May 2016. <http://www.mintel.com/press-centre/food-and-drink/us-

smoothie-market-slurps-up-2-billion-in-sales>.

Chapter 3

Face-to-Face Driver

So there you are, walking around your classroom and every student is playing Minecraft on the computer. Kids are smiling ear to ear, yet deep in concentration. Then the principal walks in...their first question, "Why are your students PLAYING Minecraft?" You can feel the heat from their tone. You can see the wrinkles developing on their forehead from the single raised eyebrow...any normal teacher would be ready to start crying. Not you though. You know that you're about to become the star teacher of the school. You explain in a calm and cool manner to the principal, how the students in your geography class are recreating the landscape and culture of ancient Greece. The principal then looks at the screens, sees the Parthenon on top of the Acropolis, the Valley of the Temples, and even olive trees scattered about! The look of concern disappears from their face, and the biggest smile you've ever seen replaces it. You not only became the star teacher in the school, but you just facilitated a perfect lesson in the style of face-to-face driver within Blended Learning.

Blended Learning can be divided into several different categories, but the first and probably easiest for teachers to get involved in is called face-to-face driver. This is where you have a teacher inside the classroom giving typical instruction, but you employ different uses of technology in your classroom while maintaining direct instruction. Basically, just making a conscious effort to sprinkle technology into every lesson you teach. If you are just beginning to use Blended Learning, this would be great for your first year using it and can be a ton of fun!

The first step of face-to-face driver style is to understand that the instruction will still be done by the teacher, in person, for the majority of time. You will deliver a lesson as usual and then have technology resources to reinforce the lesson or take it to the next level. You do not just let the online portion take over the face-to-face instruction. This usually means online/technology assignments are given after the lesson takes place. But what kind of assignments? Let's take a closer look.

With face-to-face driver lessons, the technology parts can be as creative or standard driven as you want. To be more creative, you will have to think a bit more out of the box, but both styles of lessons are beneficial because it pushes students at what they know best: technology. Let's take the lesson stated in the introduction. Let's say you are a geography teacher studying Ancient Greece. You, as the teacher, go through all the lessons on the landscapes, landforms, culture, and architecture. Then you explain to the class that they're going to recreate Ancient Greece on the computer in Minecraft! (The excitement might literally blow snot from some especially nerdy kids' nose, so have some tissues ready) Minecraft is basically Legos on steroids, and it's on the computer. You get to have a world where you build

19

everything. You build hills, buildings, lakes, rivers, bays, and volcanoes… literally everything. You build the world piece by piece and brick by brick. Once again, just think Legos on the computer, but with far more freedom on pieces and unlimited space. Reserve the computer carts for a few days, create an account on Minecraft, and set up a save slot for the class to all log in to. If you are unfamiliar with the program, give yourself a few days to understand how to create a host match for students to log in, how all the controls work, and how to guide the students in this lesson. Give the students a rubric of all the things they need to include when creating the world, and let them get creative. You can either let the whole class work together, which I suggest, or they can work separately. If they all work together, then they can have the entire world created in just a couple of days. You'll just have to set up a server and have everyone join that host and then create in the same world. Now the even cooler part, have the test of the chapter on Minecraft as well. Call out famous buildings or geographical places, and the students have to go to that place on the map and screenshot it. Kids will LOVE it! Not to mention, you'll have fun and be the talk of the whole school!

While this Minecraft example is for Social Studies or Geography, it could easily be used for other subjects as well. Think about building the setting and characters in an English story, building landform examples of the Pythagorean theorem in Math (talk about Singapore Math), and building chemical reactions like volcanoes or earthquakes in Science. The possibilities are literally endless when it comes to this idea. No matter how you use Minecraft, it is ultimately getting technology into the hands of the students to let them do what they do best: use technology. It's this use of technology that we know helps to prepare them for their future. In order for this lesson to work though, remember you need to learn Minecraft yourself! It is easy to access the program, just go to www.minecraft.com to sign up and get started on it. We'll discuss learning technology more in Chapter 6, but Minecraft is an extremely large program, and you will need to explore the program itself before you bring it to the class!

Another face-to-face driver tool that is used in my classroom is "Quizstar 4 Teachers." The majority of lessons are taught in class, but technology helps create a relatable classroom dynamic for young learners. I employ "Quizstar 4 Teachers." This is a completely free program online where you can create all of your quizzes and tests for students to complete online. You can limit the number of tries on the quizzes, the dates that they're available, and see exactly where the student went wrong. In my classroom, I have all of the quizzes for that 9-week period uploaded. They can take the quizzes two times before it becomes inaccessible. I do this so when they see their first grade, they can restudy. This helps tremendously with those concerned parents. I send out an alert text to all parents once a week that quizzes should all be done by the certain date. At least two times a week, I give tablet/computer/smartphone time to take a quiz to give them more technology time in the class, and also, in case they do not have access at home. The kids like that I give them responsibility to pace themselves, parents like the retry, and I like the ability to let them relearn before their second try. All the grading is done for the teacher to easily log it in the grade book, and I love letting the kids work with what they know best: technology.

For the next tool, think of all the science fiction movies you've seen where there's a rotating hologram image of a map, globe, body, or alien that people all gather around and explore in a full 3D turning image. Now, imagine that in your classroom! This face-to-face Driver tool is called Augmented Reality. Even the name sounds cool. Augmented Reality is where you can basically project holograms on your phone or tablet and make inanimate objects come to life in 3D! Imagine having the students color a flag on paper, scan it with their phone, and then have them tour a 3D image of their OWN flag waving in the wind on a pole! They can walk around the paper with their mobile device and see the flag in 3D from all sides on their screen! Imagine the students doing flash cards for math, and they get stuck on a problem. They can scan the flash card on their phone, and it will show how to work the problem in full 3D! They can see 3D numbers pop up, and explore the answer from different angles on their phone by walking around the numbers. This does wonders for visual and kinesthetic learners. Augmented Reality will not only make them awe in wonder, but it will allow them to see things in a different light and get help they would have otherwise missed out on. This can be used in all subjects in all grades. In lower grades, imagine students coloring the animals of an ecosystem, scanning it on their phone, and then exploring all the animals in 3D that they colored by rotating their phone! In high school, imagine the students color coding a globe of the continents, and then exploring that globe in 3D by rotating their mobile device. All the while, zooming in and out by going closer to the image. Imagine students scanning a two-dimensional heart that's converted to 3D, a 3D skeletal system, or even 3D elements to better understand molecular chemistry. The possibilities are endless of what students can scan and experience in a 3D world that would otherwise just be another picture on a piece of paper!

The best part of Augmented Reality is that it is relatively easy to get and achieve in your classroom. The easiest way is to print out pages with the pictures in 2D. Then have the students color them and download the corresponding app on their phone to scan. Finally, they will be ready to explore it in 3D. The best sites for projects like this are www.quivervision.com, chromville.com, and www.twoguysandsomeipads.com. All three of these sites have great materials to print for varying grade levels and subjects to make pictures and images come to life in 3D holograms. On www.twoguysandsomeipads.com, you can even have flash cards printed out to explore in 3D like we mentioned earlier and some of the flash cards are even explained with 3D animals! The possibilities are endless, and

It's crazy that this is available in our time. There are other resources that do not require you to print that are more commercially done in book/magazine format, but they also charge a higher dollar. At Popartoys.com, they have books and puzzles that you can order, which cover a wide variety of science and geography standards that are 100% geared to Augmented Reality. The puzzles are fresh, fun, and challenging to discover and explore with 3D holograms. The images and information are all accurate, and the kids will learn more than you ever imagined when the lessons come to life. Augmented Reality is so easy: just print, install app, and scan the picture!

In some cases, pre-made Augmented Reality may seem to have its limitations though. If you are teaching a very specific standard in very high math or science, the pre-made ones may not be as rigorous as you want. Have no fear! You can actually create your own Augmented Reality scans with the program Aurasma Studio. Simply download the app, take a picture of anything you want as the scan in queue, and then select what you want to be projected when the students scan that. This can be used for hundreds of things! Have all the math problems in their homework set up where when they scan the problem. It will show a video of you working the problem on the paper. Another example would be to have a scan-in spot on the syllabus where when parents read it. They scan with their phone, and it shows a virtual tour of your classroom right then and there! All that you have to do is film on your mobile device what you want to project and then link it to that particular spot on the page. In my classroom, I'll have pictures on the wall for students to go around with their phones to scan. Once they scan the spots, they can see a hologram or a video that I've created come to life to further explain the standards. Doing Augmented Reality this way does take a bit more effort, but trust me, being able to get so specific for all subjects makes it 100% worth it. Augmented Reality is a tool students will love, and it pushes the standards to the next level.

Another exceptional face-to-face driver tool is Study Island. Once you have taught your normal lesson, allow students to complete the associated standards on Study Island. While Study Island is not free, it is a great tool. Study Island is essentially a platform where you register your class and then assign them standards. They can review the standards you taught in class and then play interactive games based on the standards to achieve mastery. It shows you their scores as well as their struggling area, so you can know what to reteach to help them more with understanding. The platform also tracks the number of tries and focuses on missed questions to improve the students' performance. I've used Study Island for years in my classroom, and the kids love the interactive games. However, in order to win the game, they must they must answer questions that show skill mastery. Whether it is winning a race or fighting through space adventures, they are ultimately learning a standard. This is what Blended Learning is all about. Blending the standards they need to learn while integrating technology. Remember, according to researcher

Amanda Lenhart, with the Pew Research Center, 81% of teens play video games so this immediately fits the majority of your student's style. [1] This allows them to be more excited to learn, but it also allows them to use their skill set to learn quicker and prepare them more for the future. Study Island is mainly a grade 3-8 tool, but it is geared to individual state standards and for all subject areas. It can be accessed and signed up for by simply going to www.studyisland.com. In my school, you can see a clear correlation between Study Island and improved test scores. Just remember, this tool is not to teach the students the whole necessary standard, it is to supplement the teachings that you have done in class.

A similar face-to-face Driver tool like Study Island is Brainpop. It covers all subject areas in grades 3-8 and shows entertaining videos, gives quizzes, and games associated with the standard. The quizzes can't be tracked, but they can be printed. My suggestion with this tool would be to teach the lesson like normal in a face-to-face driver classroom and then watch the 3-5 minute video together. Following the video, take the quiz as a class. After this is completed, allow them to play the interactive game on their own computer/tablet for reinforcement. It's enough technology interaction to let the kids have a change from a standard lesson to see value in technology.

The next tool is very specific for Foreign Language based classrooms. After a normal foreign language lesson is taught, have a program called Rosetta Stone ready for students to use on the computers. This software can be purchased for a classroom and is the most effective foreign language tool in the world. Normal lessons in class are important, but to truly boost pronunciation and comprehension, Rosetta Stone is a must. It allows students to truly learn at their own pace and master everything. You can set checkpoints for them to meet, but they can go through the lessons as much as they want getting along the way. Every student would have headphones and a microphone to guide their learning. It comes in almost every language imaginable and can be ordered straight from their website. Any foreign language face-to-face driver classroom needs this to truly prepare their students for not only the language but also for the use of technology in the world.

For the final tool mentioned in this chapter, imagine being on a safari. You turn your head to the left and see the lions; you turn to the right and see the elephants. You hear a bird caw above; you look up and see the most majestic bird you've ever seen soaring just above your head. Well, imagine no more! This is a reality that can be achieved every day in every classroom. It's called virtual reality. I remember when I was a kid that I would sit and dream of this virtual reality. I'd imagine how cool it would be to explore places in 3D as if I was actually there. Streets of Paris, deep-sea reefs, or heck, even just other neighborhoods in the area because I couldn't drive yet! Well, Virtual Reality is finally here and all of that is possible plus more! Companies now make virtual reality visors that you put your phone into as your screen to a virtual world. They block out all the light and all you see is what's projected on your phone. You get a 360-degree view of the location you've chosen. All you have to do is turn your head to the left, and it's just like you're at the chosen location looking to the left. Look to the right, same thing. You can even tilt your head up and gaze into the sun of the virtual location! Talk about endless possibilities for field trips! There are several companies that are getting on board to provide this, but Google is in the lead. The Google app Expeditions is specifically designed for virtual reality field trips. Have every kid in the class strap on the virtual reality visor with a phone and then you're ready to literally guide them as you explore deep-sea adventures, safaris, mountaintops, and all other crazy spots around the world. It's 100% immersive, and kids will love it. Google also has street view app, which allows you to explore streets anywhere with a 360-degree view. It is very cool for smaller trips, and they have many areas fully explorable beyond the streets!

Now, I know what you're probably thinking, "This is cool and all, but I can't afford all of this on my teacher's salary!" I couldn't agree more, I'm a teacher just like you! That's why I use DonarsChoose.org. On this site you can register and start a campaign for anything you want in your classroom, and people will begin to donate money towards it. Once the goal is reached, they will ship the item or award to your school! Then you and the kids can share in the excitement of opening it together! Another option mentioned earlier is PledgeCents.com, and it works very similarly. Regardless of which option you choose, you can easily get all your Virtual Reality visors for free this way. Otherwise, the average cost for a VR visor is $20.00. Also, I don't like depending on kids to bring/use their phone in my class. That's why I started a collection for old cell phones that could have wifi. Everyone has an old smart phone lying around, and it doesn't take any time to collect a classroom set once they start donating. Be sure and clear all the data when you get them donated to just be on the safe side. Once cleared, connect them to the school wifi, and you have an entire classroom ready for a virtual reality field trip or augmented reality! Kids will love face-to-face Blended Learning when technology is integrated as a supplement this way.

While there are literally thousands of technology tools teachers can use to enhance their classroom to become a face-to-face driver classroom, let's keep in mind a large portion of face-to-face driver is still in person teaching. This means your lessons need to be interesting, have connections with students, and be relevant. If this half of the lesson is missing, the technology side will suffer as well. Just be sure that your lessons are exciting to get the excitement even higher for the technology side of things!

1 Lenhart. Amanda. Pew Research Center. April 2015. "Teen. Social Media and Technology Overview 2015

Chapter 4

Rotation

The rotation method of blended learning, which is often referred to as the facilitator, is one of the more popular methods of blended learning. The rotation method allows students to move to various stations of learning, which sparks interest and prevents boredom. A quick example of how a rotation method could be set up is that one group could view a 10 minute video pertaining to the topic or content being taught, another group could do a hands on activity or practice, another group could get direct instruction from the teacher, and another group could be working on a lab (perhaps in an augmented reality program). Once each group has completed their station, they will progress to the next station in the room. This allows students to be continuously engaged and become active learners.

Typically, the rotation model includes online learning with an app or website(s) and a combination of direct face-to-face learning as well. There are four variations of the rotation model. The four models include individual rotation, lab rotation, station rotation, and flipped classroom rotation.

Individual rotation allows students to rotate based on their own learning levels. For instance, if a student is in a history class, they could learn about World War II by starting at a station that would allow students to learn about how World War II started. For the students who can prove mastery of the objectives through a digital assessment of the teacher's choosing, the student may then move on to the next station, which could include information on the Holocaust. If a student doesn't fully grasp and synthesize the content objectives of the Holocaust, they can choose to not progress to the next station and continue to utilize more resources on the Holocaust until they achieve a sufficient understanding.

Individual rotation allows students to work at their own pace and not feel pressured to move to a new station, just because everyone else in a student's group may have already understood the concept. Students work at their own comfort level. Those who need additional time have the ability to not progress to a new station until they're ready while students who are quicker learners may advance to a new station. This is one of the many reasons that boredom is not likely to occur while utilizing the rotation model.

The second type of rotation is the lab rotation. In this type of rotation, students rotate within a computer lab, a classroom that has readily available tablets or iPads, or other devices that can access the Internet. Have several different apps or devices set up in the classroom and have students rotate until they have finished all of the different stations. For example, if you were teaching a math lesson you could have one station set up with Study Island, a second station set up with BrainPop, and a third station with Reasoning Mind. The first two stations devices are described in the third chapter, but Reasoning Mind is an amazing math supplement for a Blended Learning classroom. It has the perfect mix of interactive games and real life application for math learners. While rotating through these three stations, the students will learn more math skills, have fun, and utilize technology. Lab rotation is not only for math though; it can be used in every subject. For some of the best websites and apps used for blended learning, refer to the technology resource guide in the final chapter of this book.

The third type of rotation is station rotation. This is the most common, especially when circumstances deem that every student cannot have individual access to tablets or computers. The station rotation involves small groups of students who rotate to different technology stations within the classroom. The stations can involve group discussion, group debate, and peer-to-peer teaching, based upon what they're currently learning or have learned within the digital learning stations. This model also allows students to become adjusted to collaborating and learning to work together with one another. This is perhaps one of the most common types of rotation when introducing the blended learning model to a classroom or a school.

Finally, the last model of blended learning is the flipped classroom model. While many educators categorize the flipped classroom model as being separate from blended learning, many view the flipped class model as being a form of blended learning because students are still integrating technology learning with direct lectures along with hands-on practice.

With the flipped classroom model, lectures are viewed at home using technology, while the hands on direct practice is done at school with the teachers being a facilitator or moderator. In the book, *Flipping the Classroom*, we reference data that shows the drastic improvements that occurred at a high school in Michigan named, Clintondale High School. While Clintondale showed astounding improvements, many other schools and classrooms have achieved comparable results using the same system. If teachers are crunched for time and do not want to create their own video lectures, they can utilize the Khan Academy's pre-recorded videos that are available for nearly every subject and content standard.

Once students return to school the following day, they apply their knowledge that they received from the previous night's practice. One of the many key advantages of this model is that if students do not understand a concept, they can rewind the video and view it once again. The next day, the teacher is available to help assist students with any issues or questions that may arise. One of the contributing factors that makes the flipped model so successful is that it allows more in-class time for hands on practice, questions, and overall comprehension time. Instead of dividing the class into a hybrid of lecturing and hands on practice, all of the lecturing/face-to-face learning/direct instructional time has taken place at home, thus permitting more time for students to learn at school and allowing more time for the teacher to monitor progress and determine the needs of their students.

All forms of the rotation models allow students to have differentiated instruction that will allow the lessons to be taught from many different angles. It also enables kinesthetic learners to get out of their seats and move around. It is one of the top three forms of blended learning and one of the more commonly used methods.

The rotation Method is one of the most successful versions of Blended Learning. It allows for students to move more at their own pace and get the lesson taught as many times as they need. While it shares many characteristics to the face-to-face Driver model and many of the same tools can be used, the Rotation Method focuses more on the movement from one group to another instead of whole class implementation. Take some of the tools listed in either the face-to-face Driver chapter or this one and get started on creating a rotation lesson in your classroom today!

Chapter 5

Online Driver

The online driver version of Blended Learning is another excellent option for many schools. Within this version, there are several sub variations that can be done. Some schools allow students to set up all their classes online while other schools just allow students to have part of their schedules online. Some require students to have face-to-face interaction with their teachers while others allow every aspect remotely. Some schools may prefer to have the students complete their work in a computer lab while others may allow students to do the work at home. Regardless of how it is handled, one key thing always remains the same: It is done online to some degree. As a teacher, your face-to-face lessons are gone for the majority of the time. You now have to figure out a way for your lessons to be done online. While most school districts already have a preset mechanism for the program used online, it is still up to you as a teacher on how to present the material and calculate student success.

The pre-set program varies from school district to school district, but if you are a superintendent, you may be in need of a pre-set program. There are several great options including; Apex Learning, Aventa Learning, Blackboard, and Plato. They vary in price, but they are all are all wonderful options. They offer pre-set courses with all the standards set up and are ready for students to learn. The courses can be edited to better suit your district's needs, but the assignments, instruction, and quizzes are already done for you. If you want to create the course from scratch, the program Moodle is recommended. There you can create all of the courses on your own and have them align very specifically to all your standards. This is more work but it could save your district some money at the same time. Some districts even mix Moodle for some classes and then another online driver for other. In my district, we mix the use of Moodle along with the use of Plato. Plato is used more for online credit recovery while Moodle is used more for students who are looking to take courses ahead of time online. Some districts permit even more autonomy to allow the teachers to teach independently teach the objectives in their own style or fashion. When this is the case, I recommend going with the free program Edmodo. With this program, it allows the teacher to post lessons, quizzes, and videos in a format very similar to Facebook. This is a great site because the kids are familiar with the format already, and it is very easy to organize. The communication that is opened up between the teachers, parents, and students is also a great key feature of this free program. All of the aforementioned options are great for a fully online driven class or school. The one you choose just depends on the school district's budget.

Another site that's similar to Edmodo is Schoology. The differences between Edmodo and Schoology are comparable to the differences between Facebook and Twitter. While both sites are similar in their objectives, they are very different in design. Schoology is dually a website and an app that is available on ios operating devices as well as Android.

Schoology has an interface that is very similar to other user-friendly social media sites, such as Facebook. Perhaps one of the best features is Schoology's ability to allow students to have a maximum of 20 attempts to take a test or quiz (the instructor makes the discretion of how many attempts students can have), and once students have completed the quiz or test, they receive instantaneous feedback of their score, the questions that they got correct, and the questions that they missed. In addition to quick feedback, this site allows teachers to have more free time for additional lesson planning and other tasks necessary to help students reach their full academic potential. Schoology is great for provoking online discussions, posting presentations, make-up work, and more!

If you are looking to create your own fully immersed online course, or edit one of the pre-bought drivers, you still have to put a great deal of teaching into the class. I have taught multiple online classes varying in subjects, but yet the format doesn't need tweaking. I look at it the same way I do my normal lessons. If they are interesting and entertaining, then the student is much more likely to not only complete the lessons, but to also to synthesize and retain the knowledge being conveyed.

I present most of my online lessons in a Prezi presentation. This is similar to PowerPoint, but far more interactive. The camera whirls and twirls from slide to slide and makes the viewing experience of learning lessons much more exciting. I generally fill them with lighthearted humor as well, so that it keeps the pace of the lesson interesting, too. Now a student can't just simply read the whole lesson. Even when it's online, they still need some face-to-face interaction. One way to do this is to film oneself teaching the lesson in various scenes. Whether it is in your regular classroom, on location for topics in the lessons, or even at home, the student needs some face-to-face teaching time.

Now some people are not too keen on the idea of filming themselves. There is a solution. The app is called

Telegami. You get to create a cartoon avatar of yourself and teach the lesson over various background settings. You can create the avatar to look just like you, so it's entertaining for the students to see as well! Just simply download the app, select the scene, and record your voice for the lesson. The avatar will move just as if it was speaking! It's a great tool and students are highly entertained with it, while getting that direct instruction. So, whether it's Telegami or filming, just insert the video file into the Prezi to make the presentation more meaningful and push the students to actually do their lesson.

In a normal classroom, you need to test and quiz your students, and an online driven class is no different. In many online platforms, like the ones mentioned above, there is a system already in place. However, you can easily do your own quizzes outside of those as well. In chapter 3, the program "Quizstar 4 Teachers" was discussed, and that is one of the best programs out there. It is very easy to use and sets grades up perfectly for the grade book.

Another potential option is to add use an extremely engaging and fun website called, Quizizz. Quizizz is a trivia based review tool for students. Teachers have the ability to add visuals, such as maps, pictures, graphs, charts, etc. The students receive points based on their speed and accuracy. There is a countdown within the game that gives students the added pressure of being timed, which is typically reflective of timed state tests that students take students take in the spring. There are comical memes that are optional to appear after a student has correctly or incorrectly answered a question. Quizizz is not only fun for students, but it's a great reviewing tool.

A website that is very similar to Quizizz is Kahoot. Just the name, Kahoot, sounds like a lot of fun and that is because it is! Kahoot is a trivia based review website that allows students to review in a multiple choice format. The website also allows for a leader board to be displayed. Students work hard and strive to get onto the leaderboard. While this may seem like an informal way to assess students, it can also be a formal assessment. Data from this app can be exported to Microsoft Excel for recording data and student scores.

Often times, many online teachers forget that students who are learning online need to have just as interactive of an experience as a student in a classroom. Many of the tools mentioned in the face-to-face driver or rotation chapter can be carried on into the online driver platform to give the students a much fuller experience. Go ahead and use virtual reality field trips, and why couldn't you still do the Minecraft lesson as well?! These are great tools that appeal to this generation of learners, so use them in an online classroom as well! The students will thank you, and after seeing test scores, the principal and parents will be thanking you, too!

Chapter 6

Learning Technology

A few years back, I was at a 10k race, and I saw something unique for the time flying above my head. It wasn't a strange bird or anything like that, it was mechanical and remote controlled. It was a drone! It was literally filming the race that I was running, and you could see the footage online later that day. I. Was. Amazed. I thought I could use this to see the fields at my house. I could use this to help spot and count cattle. I could use this for SO many things! So needless to say, I purchased a drone. A few days later, the package arrives at my doorstep, I bring it inside and off to the field to fly and film! I got the propellers turning and off it goes! The first 10 seconds were awesome. It went straight up like a rocket….and then down like a rock…smashing right into the ground. Battery had popped out, grass stuck in the propellers, and it clearly had a very rough landing. What went wrong? I had seen the cool technology. I had bought the cool technology. I had a very short lived run due to luck with the technology that turned into a disaster. The problem? I never learned how to use the technology. I had instructions, I had several pages of it actually, but I never bothered to even glace at them. I just wanted the results of the technology, and I didn't want to learn first. Huge mistake. This same concept applies to your classroom when implementing Blended Learning. You can read all about this technology, see it in action in workshops, but if you never learn how to use it yourself, it will be a disaster.

Anytime you learn of a new technology, take at least a few hours to play around with it yourself first. You need to know all of the ins and outs of the new technology, because questions will obviously come up pertaining to the new technology. If your platform is a mobile device, learn how the wifi settings, structure, and operating system all work. If this basic concept fails during a class, then the whole lesson will come crashing. The number of times I've heard of great lessons failing due to wifi problems and connectivity is too many to count. The same issue can arise when using laptops for the students. Every teacher in your school should have the passwords to the wifi to truly be able to utilize technology in the classroom. Be sure to have the passwords all handy once you've learned the systems you're operating with. I keep an ongoing list on my phone of all the passwords that I might need during a day.

Once the platforms are all learned, you need to take time to explore all the apps that you are planning to use during the class. There are so many apps that require you to set up classes and put the students' information into it in order for it operate correctly. Only when it is operating correctly will you be able to track your students. The apps often times have many inventive side features. It's only after taking a few hours to truly explore the app that one can find these side features. Often times it's knowing all the features that makes the classroom experience so much better for the students.

Some apps and technology that you use in the classroom can be pretty intimidating if you don't know how to use the technology very well to begin with. If this is the case, have no fear. In-services are here! Each and every school year, my district and several nearby districts offer numerous in-services on how to use up and coming technology in the classroom. These are highly beneficial to sign up for, and you get so many new ideas for your classroom! If you need just basic computer skills to simply even get started, contact your local library or university. They almost always have technology or computer classes for beginners, which are given in the afternoons. Often times these classes are free; however, if they are not, just ask your principal if you can use room funds or if the school can pay. Often times, schools may have Title 1 or Title 2 funds that are allocated for teachers to attend professional developments. A principal knows the value of Blended Learning and would never refuse a teacher trying to get caught up on it.

One of the best ideas for learning the ins and outs of any technology you are using is to enlist a few students to help. If you ask a few students to help you learn an app, they will be ecstatic. They will learn it crazy fast (remember this is their generation's calling!), and they will show you so many things that could have taken you hours to discover. Plus, when you integrate it for your full classroom, you'll have fully trained helpers to help with the roll-out! This will make so many technology changes in your classroom go flawlessly, and you'll lift the self-esteem of those students who are helping to a new level. I like to rotate my helpers for different technology, so everyone gets a chance to be an expert and to help me learn the new technology better as well.

If you plan on using technology in your classroom, you have to take the time to learn it if you want a successful lesson. Just like with my drone, it was a disaster because I didn't want to learn how to fly it first. After I took the time to read the guide and watched a couple of videos, I'm now flying like a champ. Take the time to learn the technology in your classroom; your students will thank you later.

Chapter 7

Blended Learning: It's Not Just for the Students

Have you ever sat in a faculty meeting thinking to yourself, "We could've read about this information, watched a video, or collaborated with a professional learning community prior to this meeting, and it would've cut out half of the meeting time?" We've all been in meeting with this thought at one time or another. What Blended learning would enable is not only for students. The concept and effectiveness can be a tool that can help faculty meetings become more productive, engaging, and be more effective for the time you're meeting.

Professional learning communities can utilize various data software programs and look at the data from other teachers within the PLC. The data can be disaggregated, and by the time the PLC meeting is officially in session, the meetings will be more efficient, and all of the time that used to be spent on disaggregating and collecting data would be spent towards creating and brainstorming ideas to help students show improvement in their scores and benchmark gains.

PLC teams or entire faculties could also utilize a program s

as Schoology to upload charts that could be viewed and

interpreted by teachers prior to the beginning of a meeting,

questions could be posted on the discussion board, and a

moderator, administrator, or meeting leader could compile the

questions to be answered at the meeting. What an efficient

way to have a meeting! This would free up so much more

time for other things such as grading, lesson planning, and the

many other things that a teacher could be doing. Blended

learning techniques for adults work to cut out more fat or fluff

from meetings, and instead, focus on the meat, or the

information that's critical.

Some people say that robots are eventually going to

replace humans at a great portion of jobs. Robots can be much

more efficient, and in many cases, robots cost much less than

human labor. Let's face it, robots don't require a pension

plan, a minimum of two weeks of vacation annually, or even a

lunch break. If this is the possible direction that our world is going in, who will build the robots? Will robots be building

the other robots? While it's very unlikely that the robots will

honestly take over the majority of human labor anytime in the

near future, the reality is that technology, computers, the

Internet, and basic digital literacy is a necessity for survival in

today's modern world. This trend is just going to continue as

the years go by.

As we progress from economies that once relied

primarily on farming, logging, mining, and extracting from the

earth, society is now focused on manufacturing and the sales

industry. During the Cold War and Space Race, schools

placed emphasis on teaching students more math and science

classes in order to compete globally and especially against the

former Soviet Union. This reaction and responsiveness to

what would benefit our country and society helped America

build a strong foundation for many of the luxuries that we

have today. Today, we must focus on technology as that is

what's currently driving our world. It has often been argued that physical/tangible textbooks will soon be a thing of the past. Think about it...why should students carry around 7 or 8 heavy textbooks in their backpack? This will eventually lead to back issues. They could simply carry a laptop, Chromebook, or tablet that will allow them to access their textbooks, the world wide web, videos, and other resources/apps that will solidify their understanding far better than traditional textbooks ever could.

Digital literacy is the ability to successfully use, navigate, design, and create while using a wide spectrum of different types of hardware, software, websites, and apps. Digital learning and literacy will help students in several facets of life and occupations. At a local fast food restaurant, there was a sign that said "Now Hiring." A decade ago, that sign would say, "Now Hiring, Apply Inside." Instead, the sign said "Now Hiring: Apply at www._____.com" Whether anyone likes it or not, this is the world that we're now living in. Police offers are utilizing technology from scanning license plates as they're traveling down the road, awaiting a ping on a vehicle that has expired tags, a driver who may have a warrant for their arrest, or stolen vehicles. They also use apps that show them what type of narcotics they may be confiscating from prospective criminals. Doctors and nurses are now using computers and tablets to help pinpoint ailments and symptoms to help correctly diagnose patients and prescribe the correct medicine. Farmers are using GPS to plow, plant, and harvest crops in fields.

The average employer requires a minimum of having experience in Microsoft Word, internet navigation, utilizing social media for marketing purposes, and familiarity with basic electronic trouble shooting. In addition to teaching necessary skills required for helping enhance future skills and employment marketability, it's imperative that students understand proper web etiquette and how their digital footprint can help or harm their future prospective chances of gaining future employment. With an ever-changing society progressing towards becoming digital in nearly every aspect,

digital literacy with blended learning is not only beneficial to

students; it's a necessity.

Chapter 8

Research for Blended Learning

While Blended Learning makes sense based on a logical standpoint, many like to see direct results and researched evidence that Blended Learning is beneficial. There are literally thousands of schools throughout the United States that have seen success with Blended Learning. This chapter is going to take a closer look at five individual districts or schools from all around the United States that really showed what a difference Blended Learning can make.

First let's begin in the South. In 2004, the state of Alabama was in a bit of trouble. Its graduation rate was 61%, it was 14th out of 16 Southern states for availability on AP courses, and 32% of the students were in rural schools with poor technology access.[3] Alabama, by all accounts, was behind and needed to improve. They believed the best way to get out of their current situation was to change their state to be suited for the learners of the 21st century. They took the full plunge into Blended Learning. They created ACCESS

(Alabama Connecting Classroom, Educators, and Students Statewide) Distant Learning Program. ACCESS's main goal was to allow videoconferencing and online programs to all high school students. The price wasn't cheap though. They budgeted for $85,000 for every high school to get a minimum of 25 tablets, video chat equipment, wifi, projectors, and several other devices of technology. They were making sure every high school had at least one 21st century classroom. This was because they were ready to fully launch online classes, and they needed a place for students to take these online classes who didn't have access at home. There are several ways they do their online classes. Some online classes are video chat classes, and some are web-based instruction through programs like Moodle. Either way, they were opening the door for classes they didn't have in school for teachers to teach, such as AP classes. They were also offering students a chance to actually catch up on classes they got behind on without having to physically repeat the class. Also, several students took online classes as an opportunity to get ahead and graduate early. By 2010, ACCESS was a huge success and was the third-largest virtual school in the United States. The number of AP testers had doubled as well as the percent of people actually passing them. By 2008, the graduation rate was up to 69%, growing at the fastest rate in the country, and by 2013, it was up to 80%![4] These are crazy gains that have thrown Alabama much closer to the top in the United States. Let's not forget how they got technology into the hands of a very large percent of students that didn't even have access to it. That alone prepares them more for the future. Clearly by adopting more technology, Alabama is focusing on what kids need to truly succeed during this day and age. [3]

Next, let's look at Albuquerque Public Schools in New Mexico. Albuquerque Public Schools had run an evening program for dropouts and credit recovery since the 1920s. [3] They hosted it in the high schools at night and classes were taught by teachers in person. However, the program expanded and was outgrowing its space and was facing being shut down. To offset this, in 2009, they tried a new idea, use the Internet and technology to fix the issue. This would be geared more to what students are used to as well as preparing them for the future. By 2010, it was geared up and eCADEMY began. They constructed a small building with a lab open in the evening for the eCADEMY students. The way the school works is the students start the semester with a face-to-face meeting, and the rest is done online. During the face-to-face, they explain the course, office hours, and how to complete the course. They offer all subjects online and create the online course themselves and use tools from the National Repository of Online Courses (NROC). The courses they create are hosted through the program, Blackboard. They have truly opened the door to advancing students with Blended Learning who have fallen behind. They have had a 20% increase in retention rate as well as over 30% increase in teacher-parent connections. While this has clearly benefited the students, it has also greatly benefited the schools' budget because eCADEMY has been the least expensive school they have ever built and has helped and continues to help thousands of students. If done correctly Blended Learning can actually save districts money. [3]

Let's now turn to the West Coast for the results of a face-to-face driver example. In San Diego, the leaders began to see that there was a lack of technological training in the area. They decided to fix this problem to the max. They created eleven charter schools in the area that were highly advanced with all the newest technology with an emphasis on adult world connections and to prepare students for high tech jobs. [3] They were called High-Tech High-Schools and we're talking about kids who were literally building hover boards. There is still an instructor in all the classes, so it's not online; however, technology is integrated into almost every lesson. You have a normal lesson where the teacher shows concepts and explains the content, then you put all of that into practical action with technology. They are constantly constructing new projects and keep the kids focused and ready to be the inventors of the future. For foreign language, they also supplement with Rosetta Stone like it was mentioned in chapter 3. They believe that a year with Rosetta Stone is better than even the best in-person teacher. This school is an amazing success because of its emphasis on technology and has a 100% rate of senior acceptance into college. This is face-to-face driver done at its best. [3]

Also, in California, there is a school district called, Rocketship Education. [3] It was founded in the lower income area of San Jose. The goal with Rocketship Education is for 75% of the education be done in the classroom and 25% completed online. Basically, they work computer lab time into each school day. They use this mandatory lab time to focus on individual student needs. If a student is struggling in math, they log onto Dream Box, Reasoning Mind, and ALEKS. If they struggling in reading, they program them into Headsprout, Accelerated Reader, and Rosetta Stone. (See

Chapter 10 for more information on all the programs listed).

With this model of built-in lab time, they have proficiency

rating of 93% in math and 75% in English, which is far above

the state's average. They claim the computer labs save

$500,000 per school, which they reinvest in after school

programs and higher teacher salaries. With fewer students

being forced to repeat classes, it saves the school money while

helping students along the way. With the success, they are

continually building more Rocketship schools throughout the

city. [3]

For the final example, let's look at Wichita Public

Schools in Wichita, Kansas. This is one of the largest school

districts in the Midwest. [3] They had an issue with the drop-

out rate. They needed a method to get Credit Recovery as

well as Drop-Out Recovery up to par. They turned to

technology. It's what the students already use and will help

prepare them for the real world. They selected APEX

Learning from the hundreds of drivers out there and began.

For students who had already dropped out they created small labs in public areas like malls where they could enroll and take online classes. Each mall location had two full time licensed teachers to help and grade material. Drop-outs could come here, enroll, and either complete the courses there or go home to do it. Either way, since they are completing the courses, it allows the students to get a regular diploma instead of a GED. For credit recovery, they use the same program but allow computer labs inside the school stay open until 6pm to let students take the courses online and recover their credits. What better way to catch students up than letting them work at their own pace and with tools of their generation? Because of these programs, graduation rate has risen over 8%, and the costs of dropout students has declined over $7,000 per student.

3

When a school adopts technology in the classroom, it pushes students to their max because they are working with the tools of their generation. Whether it is enriching face-to-

74

face classes like High-Tech High-School or going fully online like eCADEMY in New Mexico, the results are clear. Students succeed when given the correct tools. Maybe it's time for you or your district to look at some of these results, and take the plunge!

3. Staker, Heather, Eric Chan, Matthew Clayton, Alex Hernandez, Michael B. Horn, and Katherine Mackey. "The Rise of K–12 Blended Learning Profiles of Emerging Models." *Innosight Institute* (2011): n. pag. May 2011. Web. June 2016. <http://www.christenseninstitute.org/wp-content/uploads/2013/04/The-rise-of-K-12-blended-learning.emerging-models.pdf>.

4. "High School Graduation Rates by State." *High School Graduation Rates by State*. Governing, 2011. Web. 15 July 2016. <http://www.governing.com/gov-data/high-school-graduation-rates-by-state.html>.

Chapter 9

Advantages of Blended Learning

Aside from being able to connect with students, enhancing students' digital fluency, and adapting lessons to incorporate technology into the curriculum, blended learning has several residual advantages. The first is the advantage of placing students into stations that will permit students to grow and succeed at their own pace and ability. This is a pedagogical revolution that allows learning to be more student centered. Rather than having to reteach concepts that students didn't understand the first time that they were taught, the blended model allows for students to be stationed into groups based upon their learning pace. All students have varying learning levels and paces in which they learn. With blended learning, teachers can set up and arrange lessons to allow students to work at a fast or slow pace which is contingent upon their own individual learning levels. Furthermore, if students don't understand a concept at first, the teacher can act as a facilitator of learning to help reinforce the learning.

Students have more flexibility and freedom to learn at their own comfort levels.

A second advantage of blended learning is the ability to dissagregate data to measure the academic progress of students. With so many great applications such as Quick Key, Socrative, Quizziz, Kahoot, and Schoology (to name only a few), students are able to get instantaneous feedback and allow teachers to check for understanding. With this data, teachers can determine which skills and content standards need to be re-taught. Several programs, such as Schoology.com, allow students to take tests and quizzes multiple times and give teachers the options of collecting a wide-spectrum of scores. For example, if a teacher allows students to take a quiz up to three times, the teacher can collect the student's highest score of the three quizzes, the average, or the very last quiz that was attempted of the three. With traditional pencil to paper tests, teachers would find themselves in a situation that would require them to live a life of non-stop grading by allowing students to attempt a quiz more than once. Ultimately, the goal of teaching is for students to fully comprehend, understand, and synthesize the material being taught. With the blended learning approach and by utilizing programs such as Schoology, students are able to reach a level of mastery without adding tremendous amounts of extra effort on the teacher. Essentially, students are able to receive better feedback and, more importantly, quicker feedback.

A third benefit is that students are acquiring technological skills, such as learning to do research online. Being online is another benefit in itself. When students are able to access the world wide web, they're able to have unlimited amounts of information and research potential, including the ability to conduct online surveys. While many students utilize technology and the internet for homework, the integration of technology and internet within the classroom enables the learning environment to be more efficient and often eliminates an excessive amount of homework for students.

Some additional advantages of the blended learning model include the ability to streamline credit recovery programs. Several school districts have set up credit recovery through software such as A+, Moodle, and Edmodo. While there has not been any long term research, it would appear that a potential effect of blended learning could potentially be an increased graduation rate. The flipped classroom models have been proven to increase graduation rates, and the blended learning model works in many of the same aspects as flipping the classroom. The difference is that with blended learning all students have access to technology. While the flipped classroom has been proven to show tremendous gains and improvements in student achievement, perhaps the greatest hindrance to the flipped classroom is that some students do not have access to the Internet, and in some circumstances, they may not have access to technology at all. With the blended learning model, technology is readily available for all students to utilize within the classroom. If accessing technology is an issue for a school district, there are several grants available for schools to introduce technology as well as websites such as donorschoose.org

With a blended learning setup, Professional Learning Communities can use universal benchmarks and use test item analysis' to determine proper steps that may be necessary to take in order to move forward with re-teaching or progressing forward with new concepts and skills. Unlike online classes, where the teacher is not on hand to help facilitate learning in person, blended learning infuses the best of both worlds – a teacher who can help with hands on learning and digital learning.

Chapter 10

Technology Resource

Guide

ALEKS – Literally standing for Assessment and Learning in Knowledge Spaces, this online tutoring company takes a student from where they are at in a course and determines exactly what a student is ready to learn. They will reinforce everything that the student is struggling with until they are ready to move on. A district could purchase this for their schools, and it would be most useful for tutoring students who are struggling. A student can complete ALEKS at home or at school and it will allow for much faster success in a classroom having this individualized tailored material at home.

Go to https://www.aleks.com to learn more.

Accelerated Reader – This is an excellent program that allows students to not only learn to read better, but it develops a love for reading. When a student begins, they take an assessment to determine their reading level, and then the teacher is able to set individual goals for each student. The goals can center on comprehension, quantity, and complexity. Once the goals have been set, a reading range is constructed where a student is to choose which books that they will read. They get to choose their own books in this range, and then take short assessments on the books that they read. Their login shows all the books that they have read, their scores, and how far along they are on their goal to move up. The students see progress while actually developing a love for reading. The newest version of Accelerated Reader now has an instructional component where the teacher can assign articles that are non-fiction for the students to read. It even shows the Lexile Level, so teacher can truly tier the assignments for individual students. This instructional component of the program helps push the students' boundaries and learn more on how to cite textual evidence when studying their subjects like Social Studies and Science. Quizzes and writing assignments are included on the instructional side of the program as well. The program is great because all of these assignments are charted and allows easy access to see where students are and how to help them grow.

Go to http://www.renaissance.com/products/accelerated-reader to learn more.

Achieve 3000 – A program that is very similar to Accelerated Reader in the aspect that it focuses on literacy. It assesses the students' reading level and pushes them to make goals and progress throughout their years in school to reach at least 1300 lexile level. It allows for grade appropriate content to be presented at every students reading levels. This helps the students get prepared for the state assessments regarding content, and it also builds stamina to make them better readers. They understand that a student's future and their college attendance hinges on their ability to read well, and it is why they emphasize it so much. The program itself is great because it allows for individual assignments for all students and gives reports and suggestions for teachers on how to take the learners to the next level.

Go to https://www.achieve3000.com to learn more.

Apex Learning – This online driver is perfect for districts that are in need of a complete system for their schools. It offers complete courses in all the core subject areas for credit recovery, original credit, intervention, or just test preparation. Once the program is licensed for your school, simply enter the students that need the online portion, and select classes that they need to enroll in. It sets individual pathways for students and allows them to revisit topics as many times as necessary to fully grasp the lessons. The program developers understand that not every learner learns the same, so they differentiate the instruction to include as many different learning styles as possible. This program is perfect for any school or district that needs a very in-depth and well-developed online driver.

Go to https://www.apexlearning.com to learn more.

Aurasma Studio - You can actually create your own Augmented Reality scans with the program Aurasma Studio. Simply download the app, take a picture of anything you want as the scan in queue, and then select what you want to be projected when the students scan that. This can be used for hundreds of things! Have all the math problems in their homework set up where when they scan the problem, and it will show a video of you working the problem on the paper!! All you have to do is film on your mobile device what you want to project, and then link it to that particular spot on the page. Doing Augmented Reality this way does take a bit more effort, but trust me, the way you can get so specific for all subjects makes it 100% worth it.

Go to http://aurasma.com to learn more.

Aventa Learning – (Recently renamed **Fuel Education**) This is an online driver that was created for districts that need a full program already in place. Much like Apex Learning, Aventa offers online classes for all grades and for every core subject. They guarantee that all of their lessons align with your particular state standards and allow for many areas to be customizable as well. Once the program is licensed for your school, simply set up your students and choose their courses. It is a fairly simple setup, and it is perfect for credit recovery, original credit, remediation, or hard to find courses.

Go to http://www.getfueled.com to learn more.

Blackboard – This platform allows for students to essentially have access to all of their classes online. It lets teachers upload their own multimedia files for students or link other files that they didn't create to students as well. Students submit all their work online, and they can see their grades and everything as well. Blackboard is a great online supplement to any classroom.

Go to http://www.blackboard.com/ to learn more.

Brainpop - Another face-to-face driver is Brainpop. It covers all subject areas in grades 3-8 and shows entertaining videos, gives quizzes, and games associated with the standard. The quizzes can't be tracked, but they can be printed. My suggestion with this tool would be to teach the lesson like normal in a face-to-face driver classroom, and then watch the 3-5 minute video together. Following the video, take the quiz as a class. After this is completed, allow them to play the interactive game on their own computer/tablet for reinforcement. It's enough technology interaction to let the kids have a change from a standard lesson to see value in technology.

Go to www.brainpop.com to learn more.

Chromville – A wonderful site to get started on Augmented Reality. It offers several pages to print out to create 3D rotatable images on your mobile device. This site is geared to Elementary School and lower High School levels. Explore the site, and it has a great deal more to offer past Augmented Reality as well! Go to www.chromville.com to learn more.

Connections Academy – This is an online driver that is free, and it is a great tool for parents to consider using with their students at home to reinforce the lessons. The courses are tailored to individual student learning styles and can be assigned through teachers for extra work to help students to succeed. This online driver is not accredited, so it cannot be used on its on for a credit; it must be used as a supplement with a teacher or parent involved.

Go to http://www.connectionsacademy.com to learn more.

Doceri – Doceri allows any iPad to essentially become a smart board that is displayed through your projector and onto your projector screen. It allows teachers to display content, and there is an area that allows teachers to use various colors to write math formulas and other annotations. It also allows teachers to record lessons and do voice overs as the problems are being worked out. These recordings can be shared with students who can listen with individual earphones and view the lessons on their individual iPads or computers.

Go to http://www.doceri.com to learn more.

Dreambox Learning – Dreambox Learning is tailored specifically for math. It assesses every student to determine where he or she is at and their learning style. From there it makes math more relevant with problems they would encounter in day to day life. It is a supplemental program that would be perfect for a rotation or face-to-face driver classroom. Teach a normal math lesson and then spend 30 minutes with students on Dreambox Learning to truly pull the student up in the gaps that they are missing content. This is a perfect software to meet students where they are at, see the real world connection, and to improve test scores.

Go to www.dreambox.com to learn more.

Edison Learning - Few companies have done so much for failing schools as Edison Learning. They focus on helping these schools have higher student achievement, but they focus mostly on graduation rates, college acceptance, and readiness for the future. They offer many online courses that are tailored for individual states and allow for customization even at the school level. While they do offer this online driver similar to the ones mentioned above, they do offer more for schools that partner with them. They focus on the life of students who are in danger of dropping out or have dropped out to help them have the life skills necessary to succeed in life.

Go to http://edisonlearning.com to learn more.

Edmodoo - This program lets the teacher post lessons, quizzes, and videos in a format very similar to Facebook. This is a great site because the kids are familiar with the format already, and it is very easy to organize. The communication that is opened up between the teachers, parents, and students is also a great key feature of this free program.

Go to www.Edmodo.com to learn more

Ed Puzzle – Ed Puzzle is perfect for teachers using blended learning or the flipped classroom model. It allows teachers to crop videos, use pre-existing videos from sites such as

Youtube to do voice-overs, and it enables teachers to create and upload their own videos. Best of all, it allows teachers to embed quizzes within the video to check for understanding. Go to http://www.edpuzzle.com to learn more.

Expedition by Google– The ultimate tool for Virtual Reality Field Trips. Have every kid in the class strap on the Virtual Reality visor with a phone, and then you're ready to literally get to guide them as you explore deep-sea adventures, safaris, mountaintops, and all other crazy spots around the world. It's 100% immersive, and kids will love it. Google also has street view app, which allows you to explore streets anywhere with a 360-degree view. Very cool for smaller trips and they have many areas fully explorable beyond the streets!

Go to https://www.google.com/edu/expeditions/ to learn more.

Flocabulary – Flocabulary uses standards based skills in hip-hop music form to help reinforce learning. We all know the power of music mnemonics when learning, and Flocabulary has pre-written and recorded songs that allow the students to reinforce the learning in a fun and easy to remember way.

Go to www.flocabulary.com to learn more.

Go Noodle – Go Noodle is a website that's perfect for teachers who live in areas that receive lots of rainstorms and snow because Go Noodle is an indoor recess app. This is perfect for hyperactive students who need to move and get their heart rate up. The site provides entertaining, differentiated physical activity songs and exercises for students to perform indoors.

Go to http://gonoodle.com to learn more.

Headsprout – This is an excellent student reading program that is made for students in grades K-5. It is developed by Learning A-Z (which is highly recommended on its own) and highly motivates kids. It is done all online and gives them a personalized online journey that gives them a story that involves them. They love the story, but it focuses on phonemic awareness, fluency, and reading comprehension. As they journey along, they become better readers while simply having fun. They offer a free trial, and it would be perfect for any rotation or face-to-face driver Blended Learning classroom.

Go to www.headsprout.com to learn more

HippoCampus – This is a great tool for teacher to use to enrich their classrooms and lessons. It offers thousands of videos, simulations, and animations throughout all the core subjects. They can use it during their lessons for technology implementation, or assign homework within it to enrich their lessons while the student is at home. All of their multimedia is designed for easy access for students, and it allows students to truly review the lessons over again in the way that a teacher would have presented it. It is perfect for all aspects of Blended Learning classrooms.

Go to http://www.hippocampus.org to learn more

Kahoot – Just the name, Kahoot, sounds like a lot of fun, and that's because it is! Kahoot is a trivia based review website that allows students to review in a multiple choice format. The website also allows for a leader board to be displayed, and while this may seem like an informal way to assess students, it can also be a formal assessment. Data from this app can be exported to Microsoft Excel for recording data and student scores.

Go to www.getkahoot.com to learn more.

K12 – This is a powerful online school that allows for students to enroll for course for help as well as for schools to use it for their coursework. It is individualized for every state and meets all the state standards that are required. When utilized as a full online driver, the program has the entire course laid out for the student. All schools or districts would need to do is complete the forms for the necessary licenses, and then enroll the students for complete online education. It allows for original credit, credit recovery, and just remediation in general. It is a great online tool that many states use.

Go to http://www.k12.com/ to learn more.

Minecraft - Minecraft is basically Legos on steroids, and it's on the computer. You get to have a world where you build everything. You build hills, buildings, lakes, rivers, bays, and volcanoes... literally everything. You build the world piece by piece and brick by brick. Once again, just think Legos on the computer, but with far more freedoms on pieces and unlimited space. It can be used with almost all subjects on having students recreate areas from history, reading, math, or science.

Go to www.minecraft.com to learn more.

Moodle – An online driver where teachers get to create their own course work. Teachers create the assignments, quizzes, and everything. It allows for ultimate control of teachers and for students to be able to take their classes online.

Go to https://moodle.org to learn more.

Plato – This is a wonderful online driver that districts can purchase a license to use. It allows for credit recovery or original credit, and it is highly tailored to individual student needs. It is aligned with each state's standards, and all of the course work is done as far as lessons and tests go. Simply assign the student the course and they complete it on their own time to receive a credit.

Go to https://ple.platoweb.com to learn more.

Popar - At Popar, they have books and puzzles you can order over all sorts of science and geography standards that are 100% geared to Augmented Reality. The puzzles are fresh, fun, and challenging to discover and explore with 3D holograms. The images and information are all accurate, and the kids will learn more than you ever imagined when they come to life.

Go to https://popartoys.com to learn more.

Prezi – A great program that will allow you to create interactive and entertaining presentations for your students. It is similar to PowerPoint, but the students will enjoy it far more and it is easier to use and upload.

Go to www.Prezi.com to learn more.

Quick Key – Quick Key is a tool that is beneficial for classes that do not have access to one-on-one Chromebook, a bring your own device policy, or a heavy amount of technology readily available and on hand. Teachers can print blank test sheets on Quick Key's website for students to use. The teacher will then download the Quick Key app, which is available for mobile devices. After the teachers has created a test bank, the students will take the test and with a quick scan of each test sheet. Teachers can give instant feedback to students and even break down the entire classes results and view a test item analysis. This analysis will show the instructor which skills and content may need to be retaught.

Go to http://www.quickkey.com to learn more.

Quiver Vision – This is a great site to get started on Augmented Reality. It offers several pages to print out to create 3D rotatable images on your mobile device. This site is geared more to the younger grades, but it is great for getting them involved with learning and technology!

Go to www.quivervision.com to learn more.

Quizizz - Quizizz is a trivia based review tool for students. Teachers have the ability to add visuals, such as maps, pictures, graphs, charts, etc. The students receive points based on their speed and accuracy. There is a countdown within the game that gives students the added pressure of being timed, which is typically reflective of timed state tests that students take students take in the spring. There are comical memes that are optional to appear after a student has correctly or incorrectly answered a question. Quizizz is not only fun for students; it's a great reviewing tool.

Go to http://www.quizizz.com to learn more.

Quizstar 4 Teachers - This is a completely free program online where you can create all of your quizzes and tests for students to complete online. You can limit the number of tries on the quizzes, the dates it's available, and see exactly where the student went wrong. It is one of the best online programs for creating quizzes to give students online.

Go to www.quizstar4teacher.com to learn more.

Reasoning Mind – The ultimate math supplement for a Blended Learning Classroom. It is designed for math grades 2-7, and it has the perfect mix of interactive games and real life application for math learners. It takes the student where they are at and pushes them in skills that will help to advance them to the next level.

Go to https://www.reasoningmind.org to learn more.

Rosetta Stone - This tool is very specific for Foreign Language based classrooms. After a normal foreign language lesson is taught, have this program ready for students to use on the computers. This can be purchased for an individual classroom. This is the most effective foreign language tool in the world. Yes, normal lessons in class are important, but to truly boost pronunciation and comprehension, Rosetta Stone is a must. It allows students to truly learn at their own pace and master everything. You can set checkpoints for them to meet, but they can go through the lessons as much as they want getting there. Every student would have headphones and a microphone to guide their learning. It comes in nearly any language imaginable, and it can be ordered straight from their website. Any foreign language face-to-face driver classroom needs this to truly prepare their students for not only the language but also for the use of technology in the world.

Go to http://www.rosettastone.com to learn more

Schoology – Schoology is dually a website and an app that is available on ios operating devices as well as Android. Schoology has an interface that's very similar to other user-friendly social media sites such as Facebook. Perhaps one of the best features is Schoology's ability to allow students to have a maximum of 20 attempts to take a test or quiz (the instructor makes the discretion of how many attempts students can have), and once students have completed the quiz or test, they receive instantaneous feedback of their score, the questions that they got correct, and the questions that they missed. In addition to fast feedback, this allows teachers to have more free time for additional lesson planning and other tasks necessary to help students reach their full academic potential. Schoology is great for provoking online discussions, posting presentations, make-up work, and more!

Go to http://www.schoology.com to learn more.

Splash Math – Splash math is designed for grades 1-5 and is a video game based website that allows students to reinforce math skills and content. The site allows students to progressively work on more complicated problems as they refine and master content. In addition to this fun and vividly colorful learning tool, students are also able to collect points as they solve equations. These points can be used towards collecting digital animals and marine life, which can be added to a digital aquarium or jungle. The students strive to have as many animals and diversity in the aquarium and jungle as they possibly can.

Go to http://www.splashmath.com to learn more.

Study Blue – Study Blue has many different facets of learning tools, but perhaps the most impressive feature is the digital notecards option. Students can create their own note cards or they have the option of studying other note cards that have been created. This is a great feature because students do not have to worry about keeping up with their own physical/tangible set of notecards with terms and definitions. Instead, with Study Blue, the notecards are readily available. If a student is riding to school on the bus and decides to take the initiative to study, they can access their set of cards and study. Additionally, they can quiz themselves, and Study Blue will compile a list of their electronic note cards that they still need to work on mastering.

Go to www.studyblue.com to learn more.

Study Island - Study Island is basically a platform where you register your class, and then assign them standards. They can review the standards you taught in class, and then play interactive games based on the standards to achieve mastery. It shows you their scores, as well as their struggling area, so you can know what to reteach and help them more. The platform also tracks the number of tries and focuses on missed questions to improve the student performance. I've used Study Island for years in my classroom, and the kids love the interactive games. However, while they play the game, in order to win, they must answer questions that show skill mastery. Whether it is winning a race or fighting through space adventures, they are ultimately learning a standard. This is what Blended Learning is all about: Blending the standards they need to learn with technology. Study Island is mainly a grade 3-8 tool; however, it is geared to individual state standards and for all subject areas.

Go to www.studyisland.com to learn more.

Teachers Pay Teachers – Teachers Pay Teachers is a great technology resource for two reasons. The first is that it allows teachers to find amazing lessons from other teachers. Some of the lessons are free while others do cost a small fee, but if you're in a bind or just looking for something that's new and refreshing for your classroom, Teachers Pay Teachers could be exactly what you've been looking for. On the other side of the coin, you can upload your own lesson ideas or unit plans to the site and sell them to other teachers who are seeking further resources. There are several success stories, but perhaps one of the more well known users is a teacher named Deanna Jump. Deanna Jump has become a millionaire selling her lessons on Teachers Pay Teachers. I know what you're thinking…."There's no way that this could be possible." Seriously, Google or Bing her name, and you can read all about her success story.

Go to www.teacherspayteachers.com to learn more.

Telegami – This is the best way to implement videos of yourself into an online presentation without having to film yourself. You get to create a cartoon avatar of yourself and teach the lesson over various background settings. You can create the avatar to look just like you so it's entertaining for the students to see as well! Just simply download the app, select the scene, and record your voice for the lesson. The avatar will move just as if it was speaking! It's a great tool, and students are highly entertained with it while getting that direct instruction.

Go to www.Telegami.com to learn more.

Too Noisy - It's all too often that teachers will request for their students to "not get too loud." But the question is, what is too loud? Every teacher may have a different definition of what too loud is and also, each student may also have their own unique interpretation. Because of this, Too Noisy is an app that enables teachers to adjust the sensitivity levels of their microphone on a phone, tablet, or computer microphone, and the app displays on a projector screen with a meter and a happy face. If the class is at a comfortable sound level, the face is happy, and the meter is in the green. If the class becomes noisy, the meter will go into the yellow or red and the happy face will become sad. It gives a great visual representation of if the class is going beyond the expected noise level or not.

Go to www.toonoisyapp.com to learn more.

Two Guys and Some Ipads – This is a phenomenal Augmented Reality site where it not only offers pages to print out for 3D images, but it also offers math flash cards in 3D and so much more!

Go to www.twoguysandsomeipads.com to learn more.

96488422R00067

Made in the USA
Columbia, SC
01 June 2018